I0753301

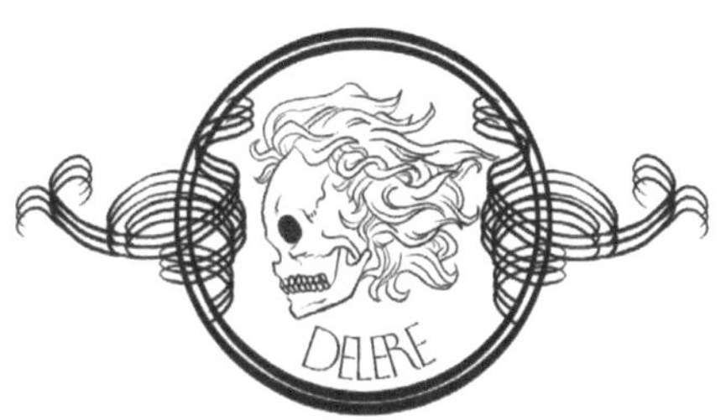
DELERE

THIS PAPERBACK EDITION 1ST PUBLISHED
IN 2017 BY DELERE PRESS LLP

◇◇

RESIDUE © VINCE BRIFFA
WHAT MATTER WHO'S SPEAKING
© JONATHAN BENNETT BONILLA

* * *

FIRST PUBLISHED IN 2017 BY
DELERE PRESS LLP
BLOCK 370G ALEXANDRA ROAD
#09-09 SINGAPORE 159960
WWW.DELEREPRESS.COM
DELERE PRESS LLP REG NO. T11LL1061K

◇◇

ALL RIGHTS RESERVED

◇◇

ISBN 978-981-11-2672-7

WHAT MATTER WHO'S SPEAKING

JONATHAN BENNETT BONILLA

RESIDUE

VINCE BRIFFA

DELERE PRESS

TO LAURA, WHO LOVES UNCONDITIONALLY
AND IS THERE, ALWAYS

VINCE BRIFFA

IN MEMORIAM C.M.F.

JONATHAN BENNETT BONILLA

WHAT MATTER WHO'S SPEAKING

JONATHAN BENNETT BONILLA

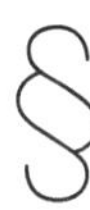

NOTHING IS SAFE

Nothing is safe.

Thoughts not said but thought.

Saying unthought

While thinking forges ahead.

Silence eternal before

FOR ANTI-CLIMACUS

For Anti-Climacus

One must give way to all things possible

Breath is prayer

Double-movement from impossibility to possibility.

All things are breathed into being

Made possible by the breath they withhold.

For Anti-Climacus

One who possesses too much possibility is in need of impossibility

One who possesses too much impossibility is in need of possibility.

Seek the body of greatest resistance. [1]

WHAT MATTER

What remains in the stack of books

is what can go for the time being left unsaid.

The author speaks

from inside the chasm of uninhabited tense

to the inhabited tense of the reader.

What matter who's speaking. [2]

CAPACITY NOT TO

Facticity of things happening is incontestable.

What of the negative potential (*potentiality to not-be*) of a thing?

Does it reflect negatively on impotential when it doesn't come to be?

That it would have the capacity to resist becoming counts for something.

One isn't what one has been.

From what one has been one can't predict what one actually will be.

What one actually will be includes one's impotential.

The capacity to not be is not the same as the capacity not to.

THRESHOLD

Becoming is origin and destiny meeting.

Everliving present you inhabit inhabits you.

In each and every now-instant it's what you're dis-inhabiting

Chamber you're stepping out of

Threshold you've walked through

Which when you turn around

You're still standing inside of.

NEGATIVE CAPABILITY

Negative Capability

Ability in spite of not-being-able

When is an accident not an accident?

When things happen can we say of them that they might not have been?

Having been

Not having been there but appearing to have

*

It

*

Asterisque

Light and hollow

Lightless supernovae

Words like nothingness words return to

Silence between silence between silence

§§

SPEECH SET FREE

Writing punctuates silence

Not the other way around.

Speech set free interrupts.

Writing silences speech.

Silence swallows what's spoken between.

RHIZOME

The book is eternal.

It comes from what shall be and what was.

The book opens out from and into the open

Twisted rhizome of cold metal and air

The book is never closed.

The book unfolds into the future tense.

What's done is never finished.

NIHILISM

Belief is arrived at by way of unbelief.

Life is what one must die into

What one must give oneself over to.

In order to give oneself one's life

One first must lose it.

Nihilism is a stage

A dying into belief for the life which is given

Breath by breath in its place.

NOISE

Unsayables trace the perimeter of the unsaid said.

Where saying falls silent nothing can be.

Saying says all the way up to where it falls silent

Saying frames the unsayable

Unsaids frame the said.

Without silence saying would sound like noise.

IT HAS THEM

Saying is inexhaustible.

You mean to exhaust it.

What speakers of language

don't know is that

they don't have language

but it has them.

BLACK LIGHT

Black light appears black due to the density of light.

Black light appears black because it's illuminated.

Black speech speaks concerning that which one cannot.

Black speech is necessary only when one cannot speak

except concerning what is not light.

Black speech must be spellbinding

in order to speak beyond the visible limit.

WHAT MATTER

You can't be certain what it is to write while writing.

While writing, writing remains *a question.*

What matter who's speaking

A third null voice? A void (   )?

null ∅

void (   )

That which cannot be said cannot be said that which cannot be said cannot be said
That which cannot be said cannot be said that which cannot be said cannot be said
That which cannot be said cannot be said that which cannot be said cannot be said
That which cannot be said cannot be said that which cannot be said cannot be said

§§§

ROSE WITHIN

Where do you go to visit the dead?

To sleep ⊃ to die ⊃ to wake ⊃ to dream

Chuang Tzu is a butterfly dreaming he's a man?

Chuang Tzu is a man dreaming he's a butterfly?

A rose is a rose is a rose is a rose.

Poem in a room sealed shut. [4]

DARK FIELD

The book is a infinite circle whose circumference is nowhere

and whose center is everywhere.

. . . all earthly existence must ultimately be contained in a book.

. . . one does not write luminously on a dark field . . .

. . . meditating without leaving any traces becomes evanescent . . .[5]

NON-LIVED

Non-lived experience ≈ life not experienced

Time of no time ≈ time of the dream

Non-lived ≈ hasn't been made known

Particles that make up Saturn's rings

Only ever ≠ ever only

Always only ≈ only ever

Fire in excess consumes the subject

Time is intractable

No getting back what you have lost.

WHAT MATTER

Death of the Author ∪∩ Birth of the Author

To tell the truth most persuasively

You must pretend that you're not lying.

Hesitation shatters the truth.

What matter who's speaking, someone said,

What matter who's speaking. [6]

DOUBLE MOVEMENT

Circulation ≈ instance of double movement

Sucking-spitting ≈ attractive-repulsive force

≈ tidal currents at the moon's command

≈ not sayable ≈ unsayable ≈ non-sayable

Oh farther than everything.

Oh farther than everything.

At the center of which

Gravity of some absence sucks you out to sea

Towards the high water mark.

It is the hour of departure.

Oh abandoned one! [7]

SILENCE KEEP

Sound echoing in the cavity of thought * without speech

Speech interrupts silence.

Speech punctuates silence not the other way around.

Silence never arrives

There is always something more to say.

Where everything has already been said, saying shapes silence.

Silence keep silence keep silence keep silence keep silence keep silence keep
silence keep silence keep silence keep silence keep silence keep silence keep

SILENTIALISTS

Not until after you've spoken can you turn back.

Language thought * is magic

What we cannot speak about we must pass over in silence.

To not speak withholds a power which is equal and opposite to speech.

Silentialists think ceaselessly. [8]

RESIDUE

VINCE BRIFFA

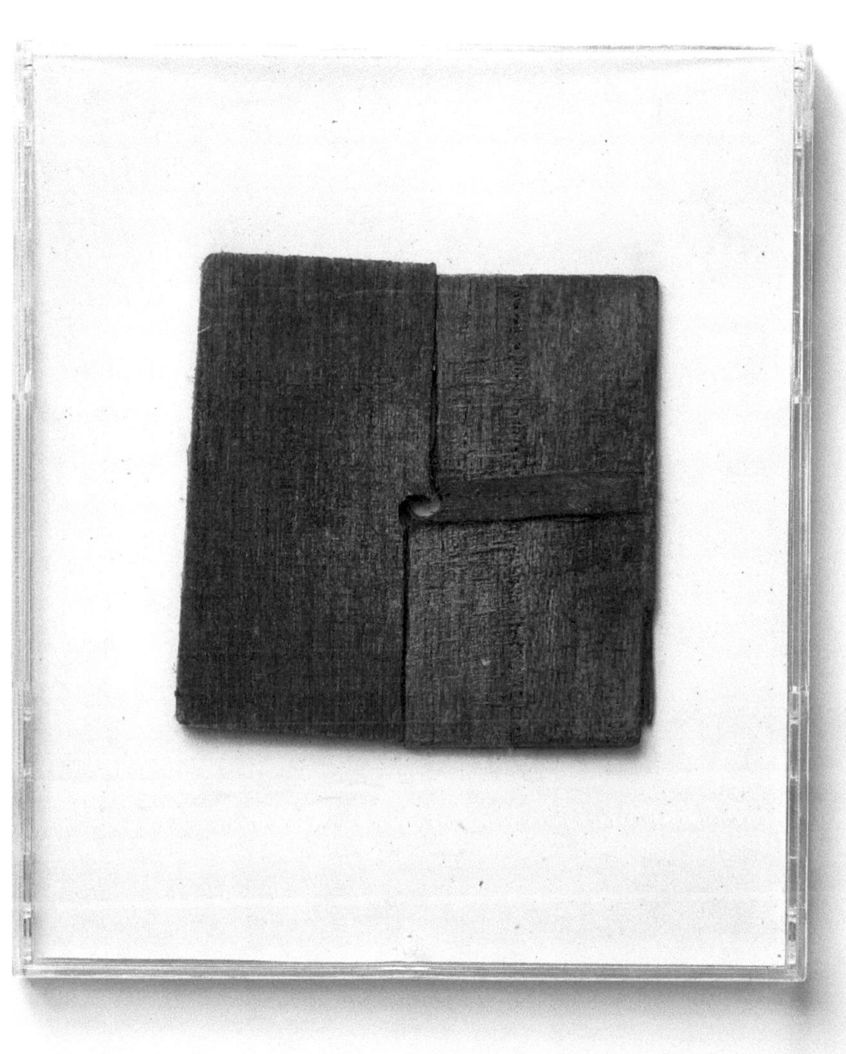

RESIDUE

(ongoing series)

VINCE BRIFFA

The series reconsiders discarded traces of a work process, remnants salvaged from my studio. RESIDUE sits at the junction between painting and objet trouvé, and is an ongoing attempt at recontextualising materiality to create new meaning. Its maxim is the strict regime of modular reasoning - for a unit to be created, the rescued has to sit well within the frame of the jewel case.

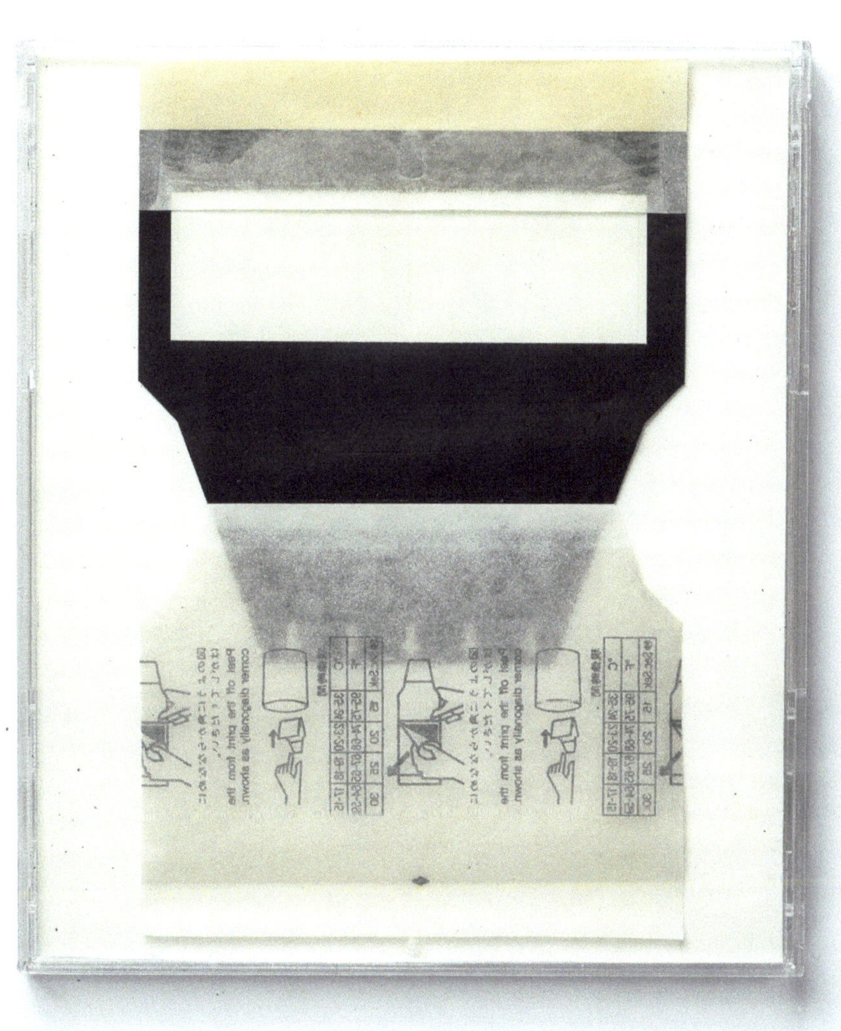

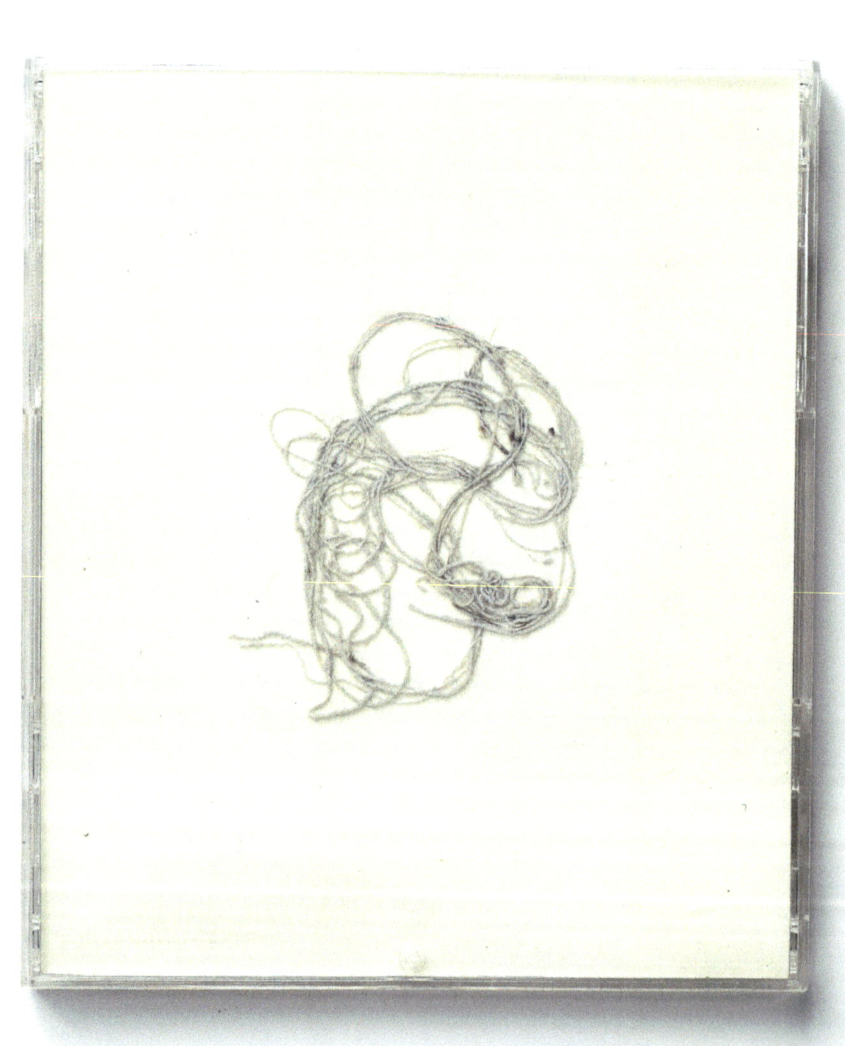

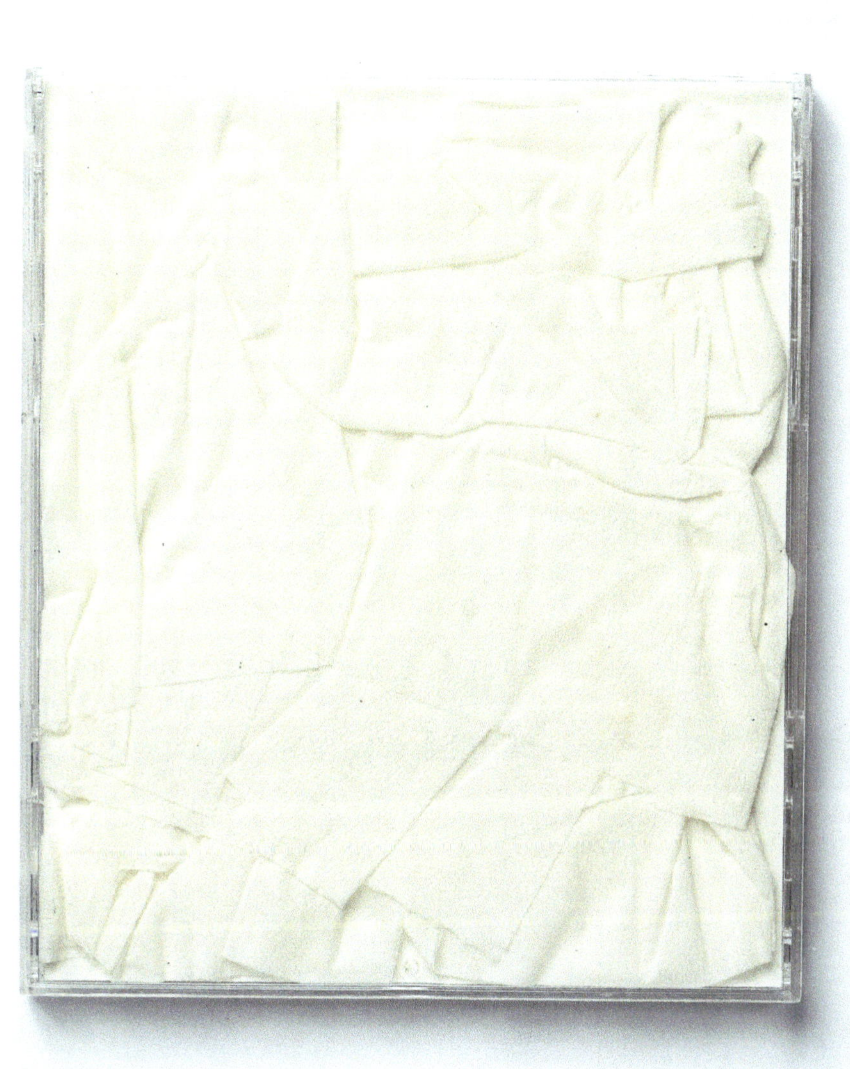

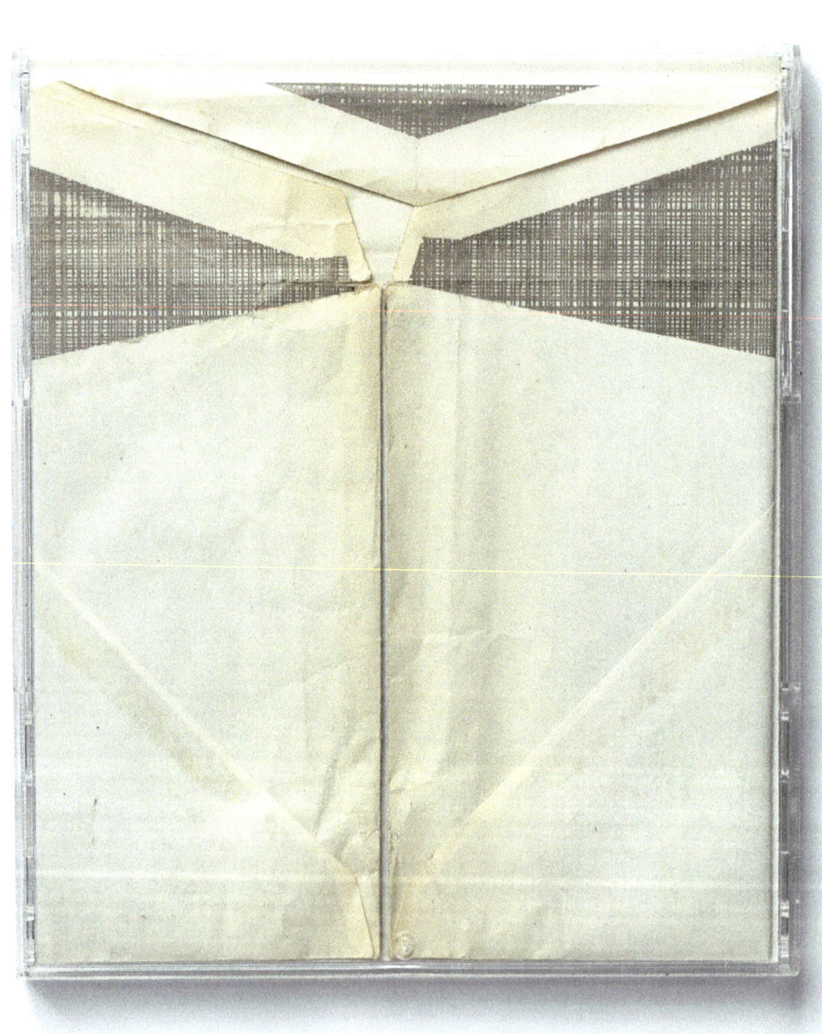

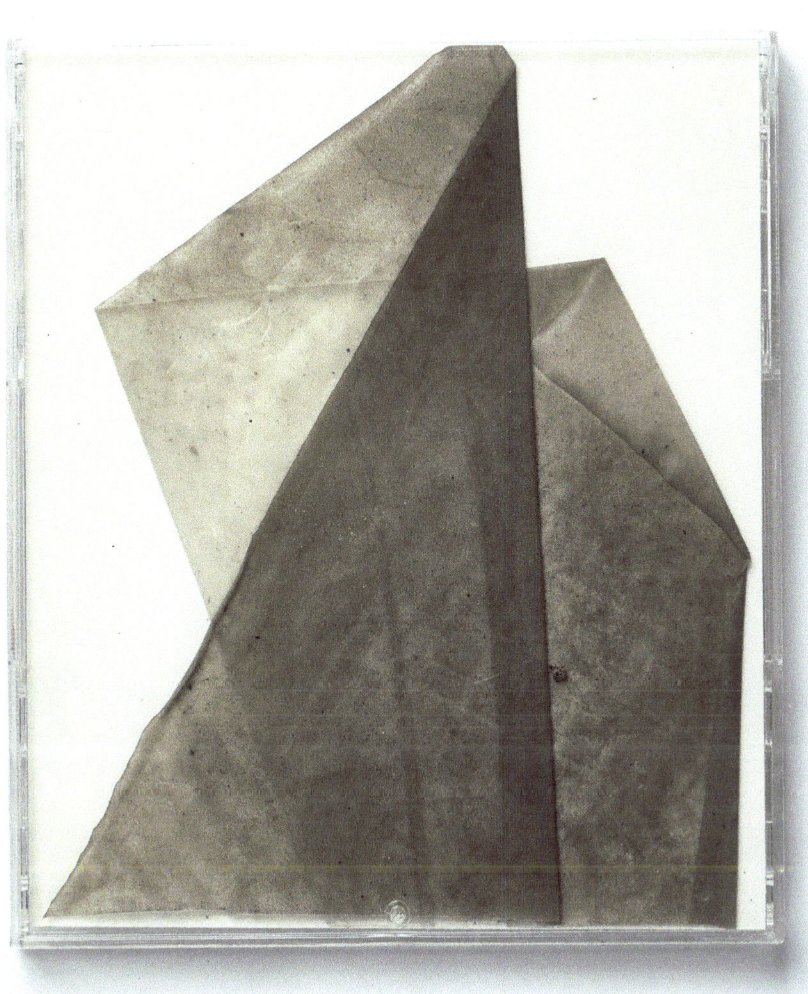

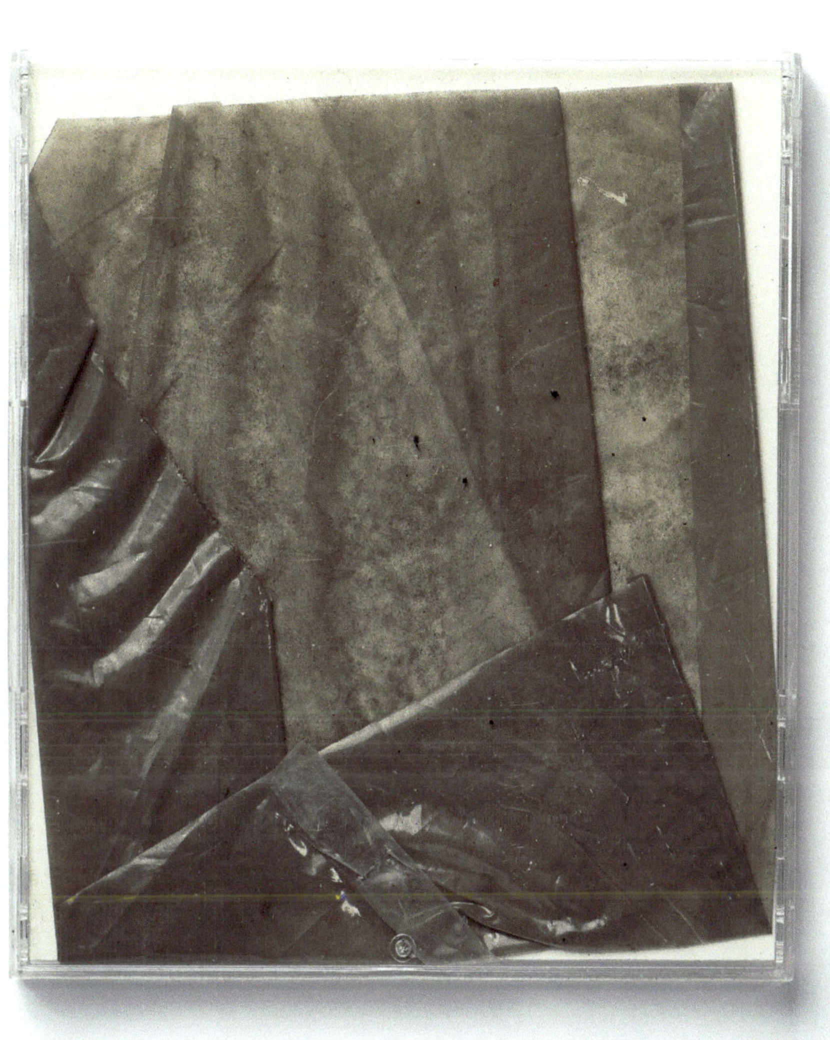

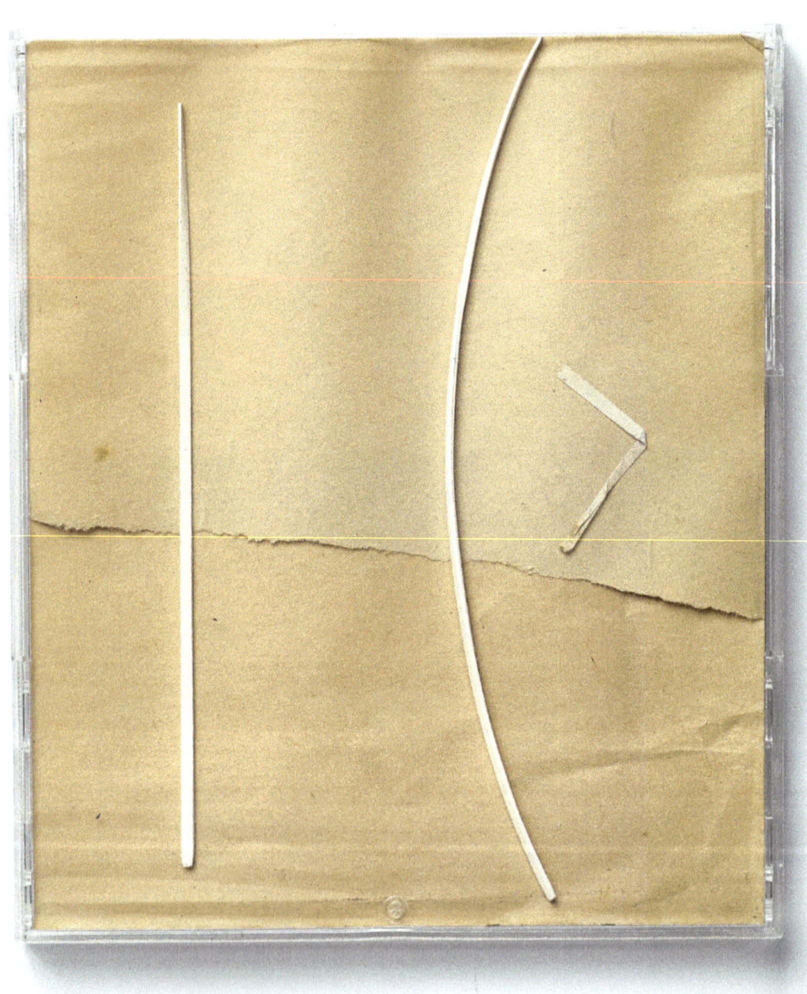

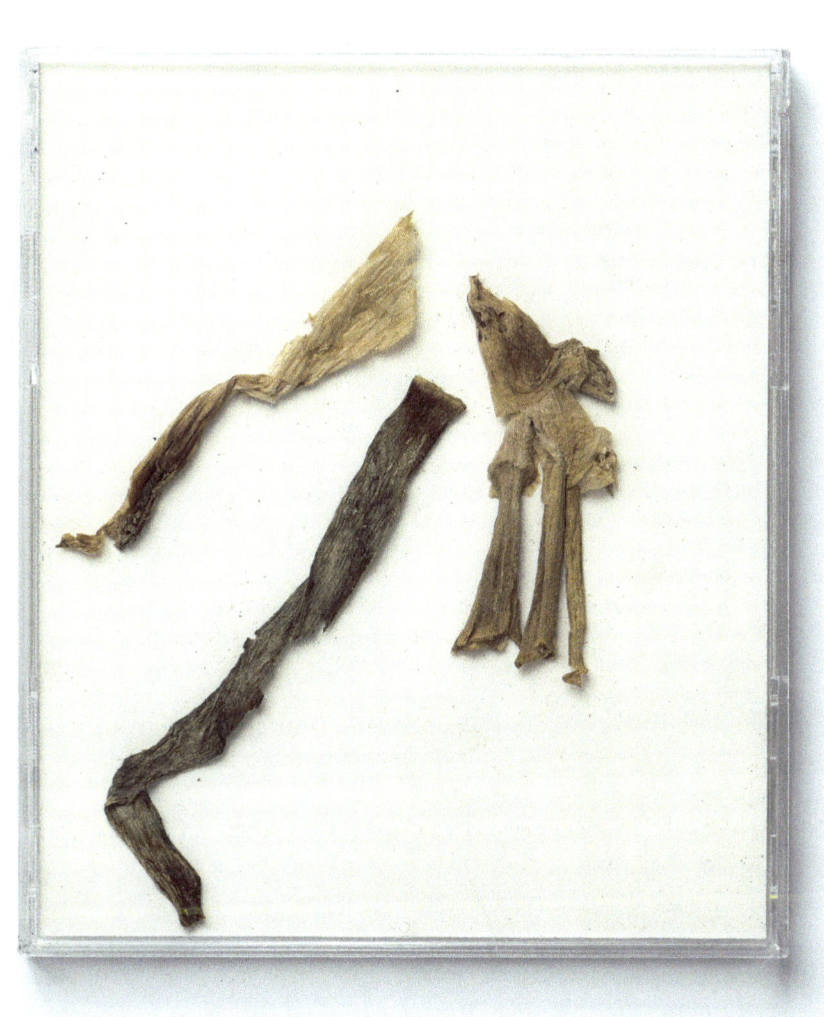

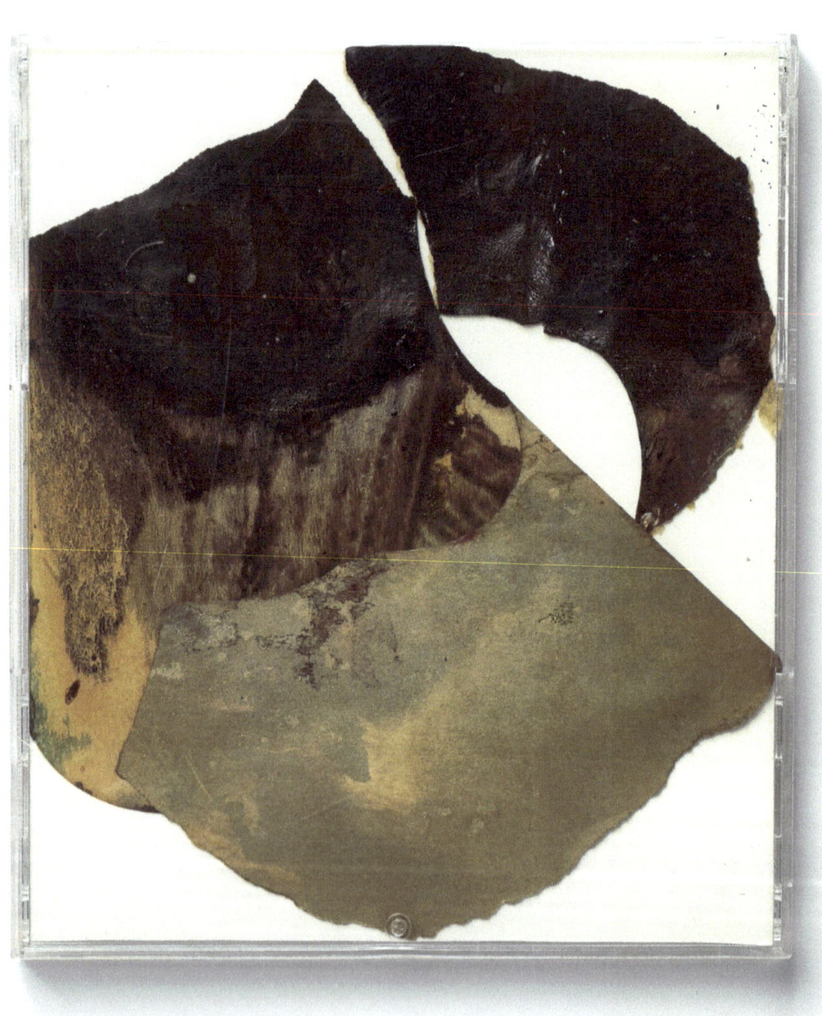

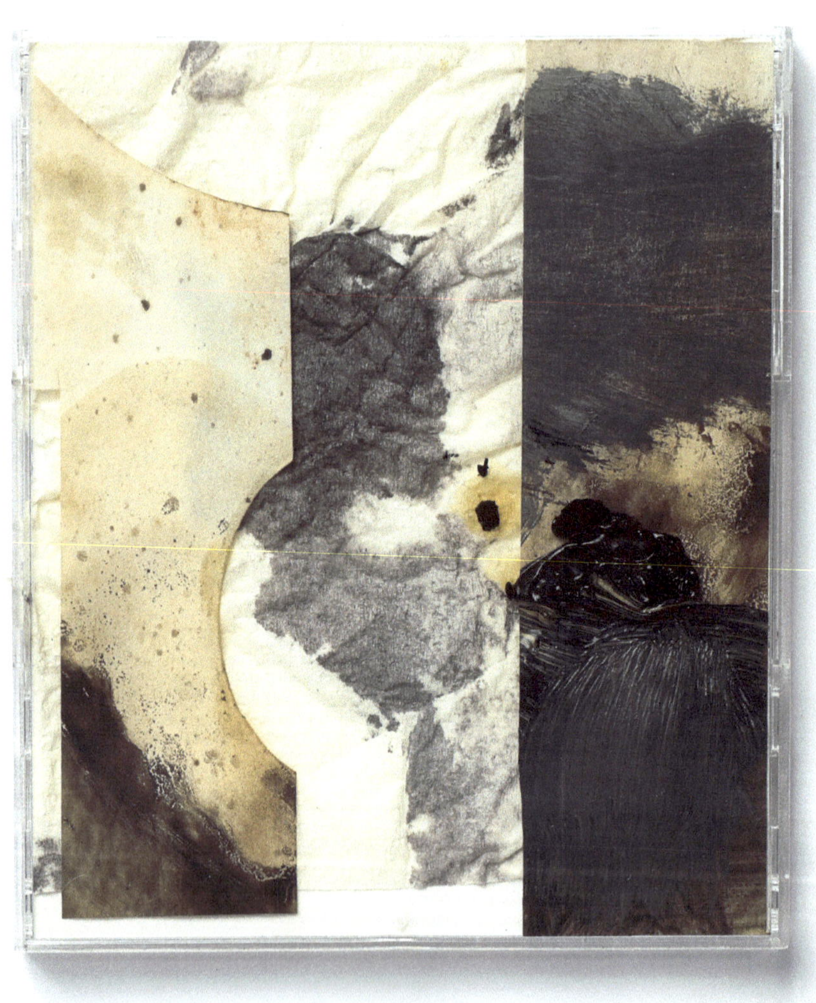

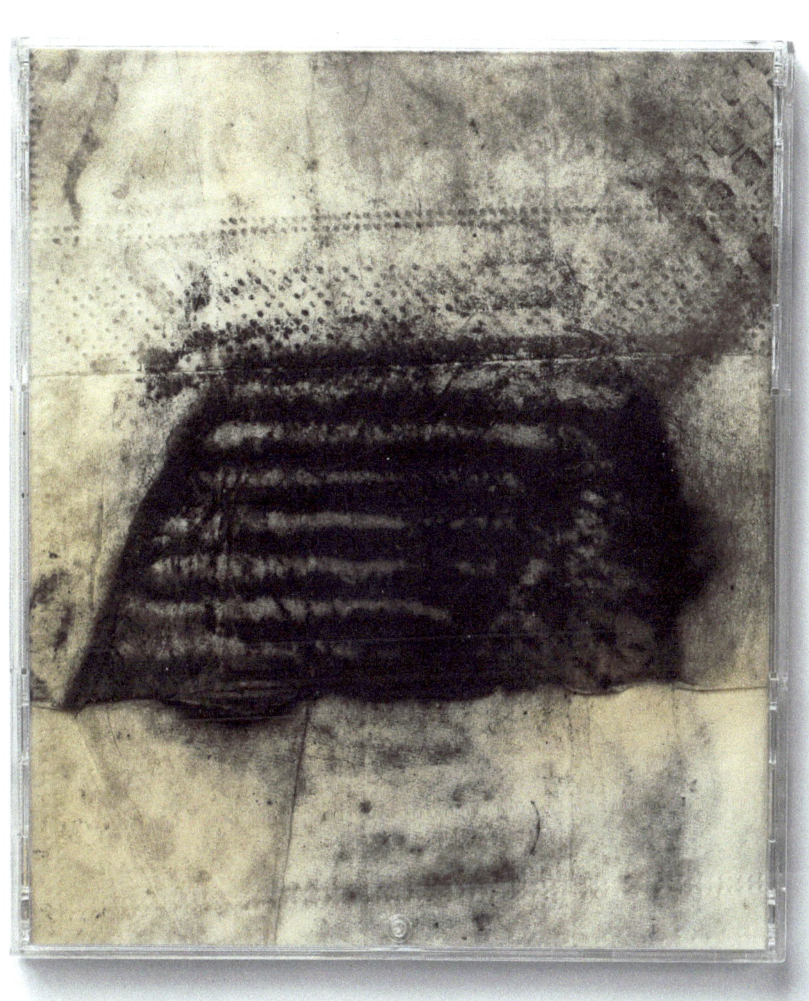

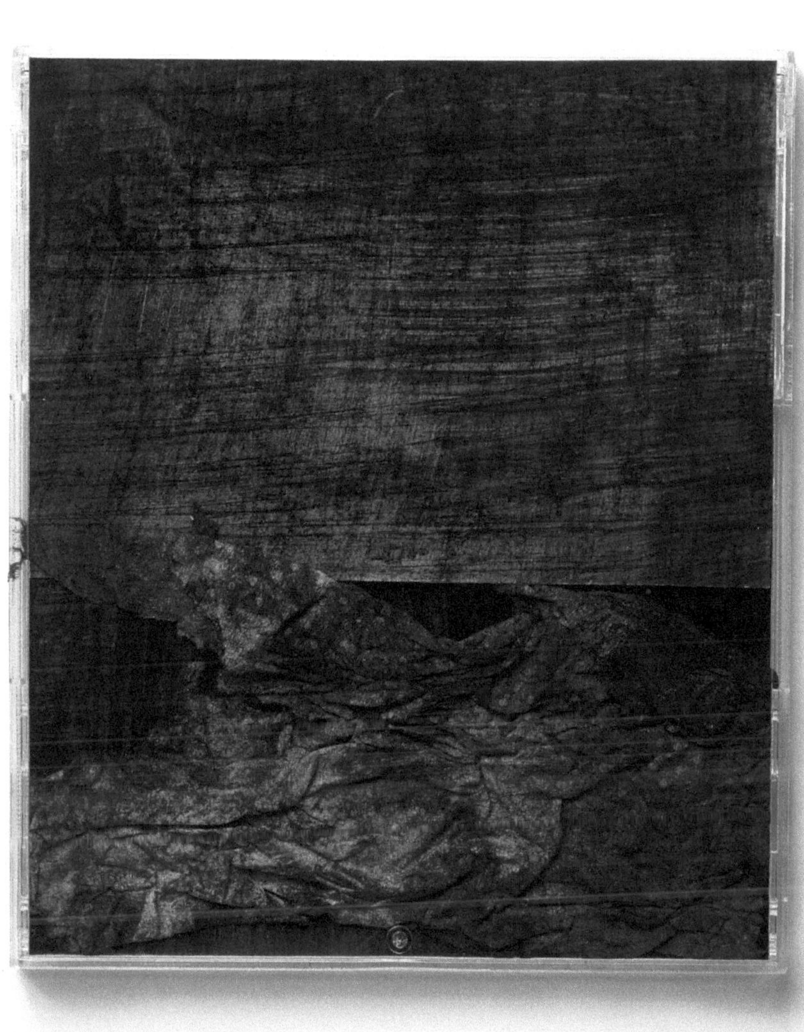

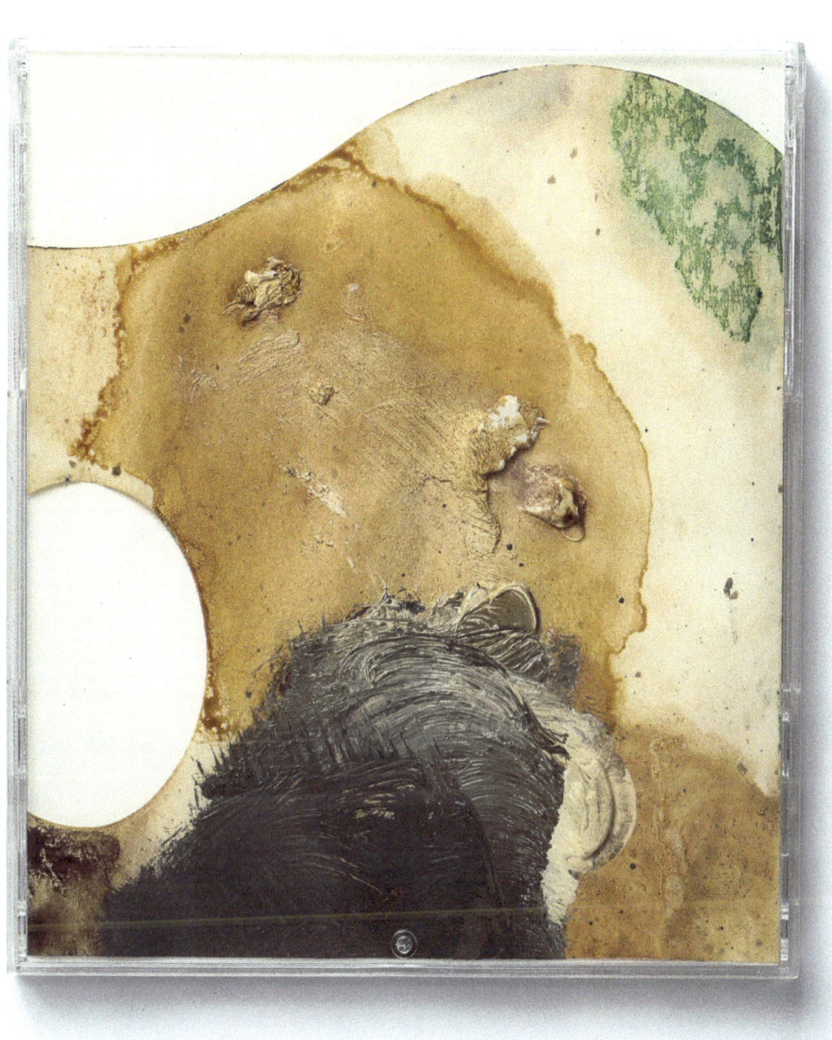

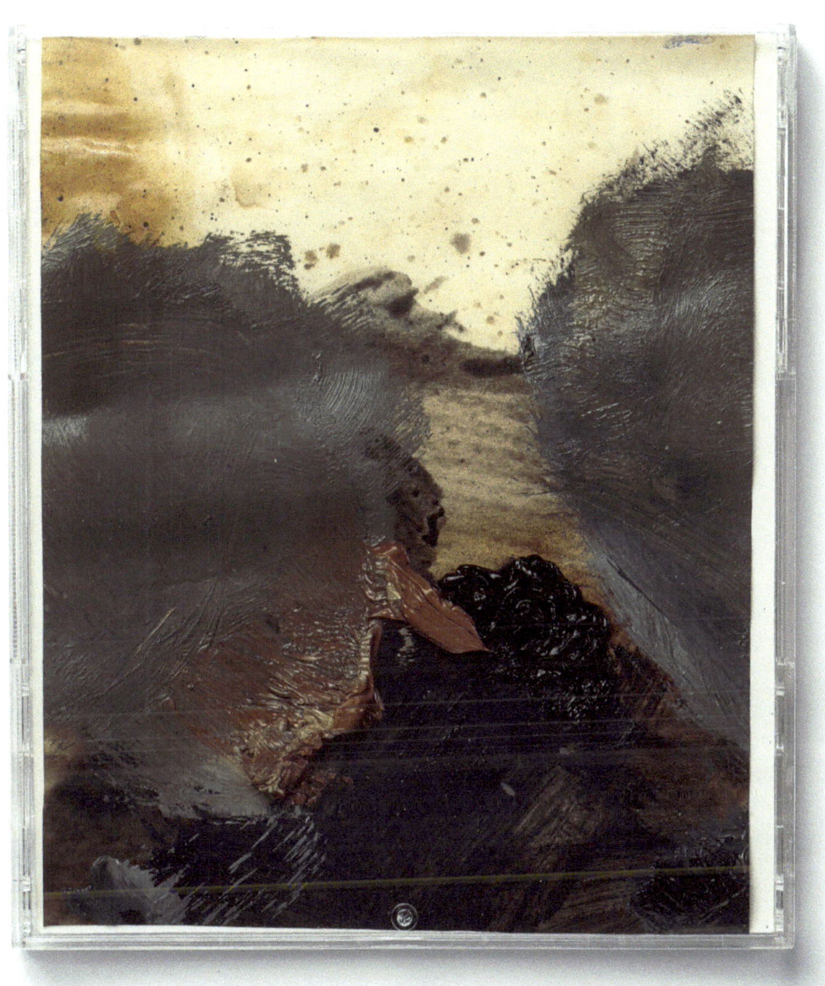

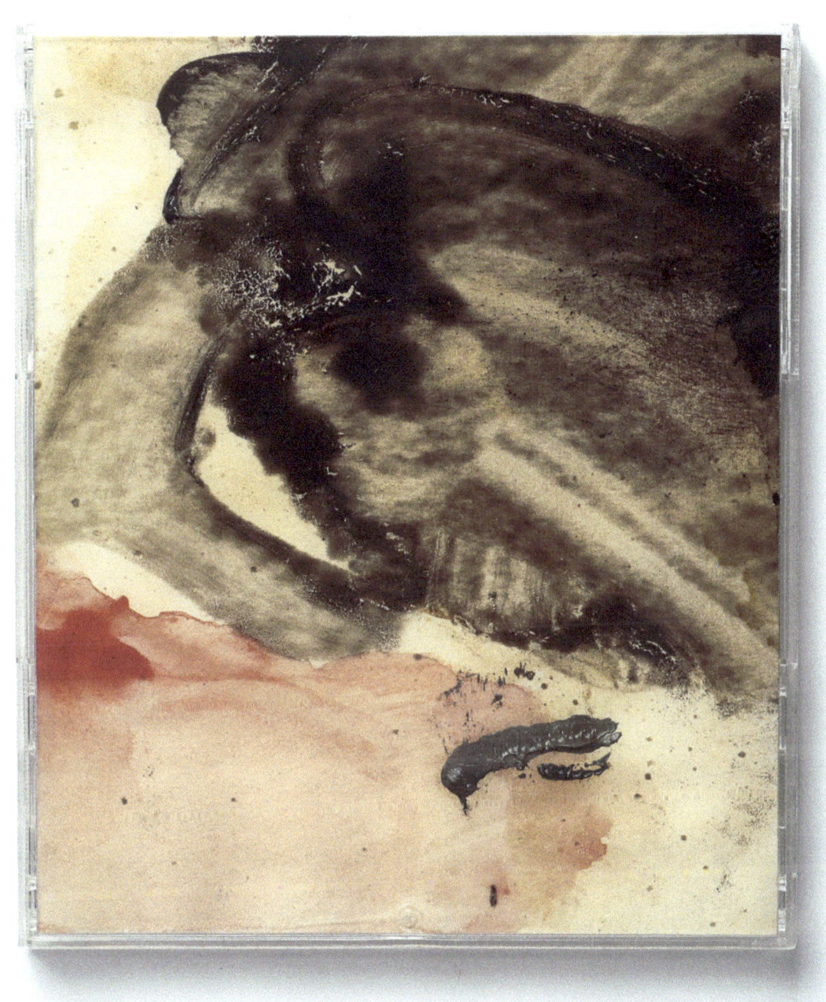

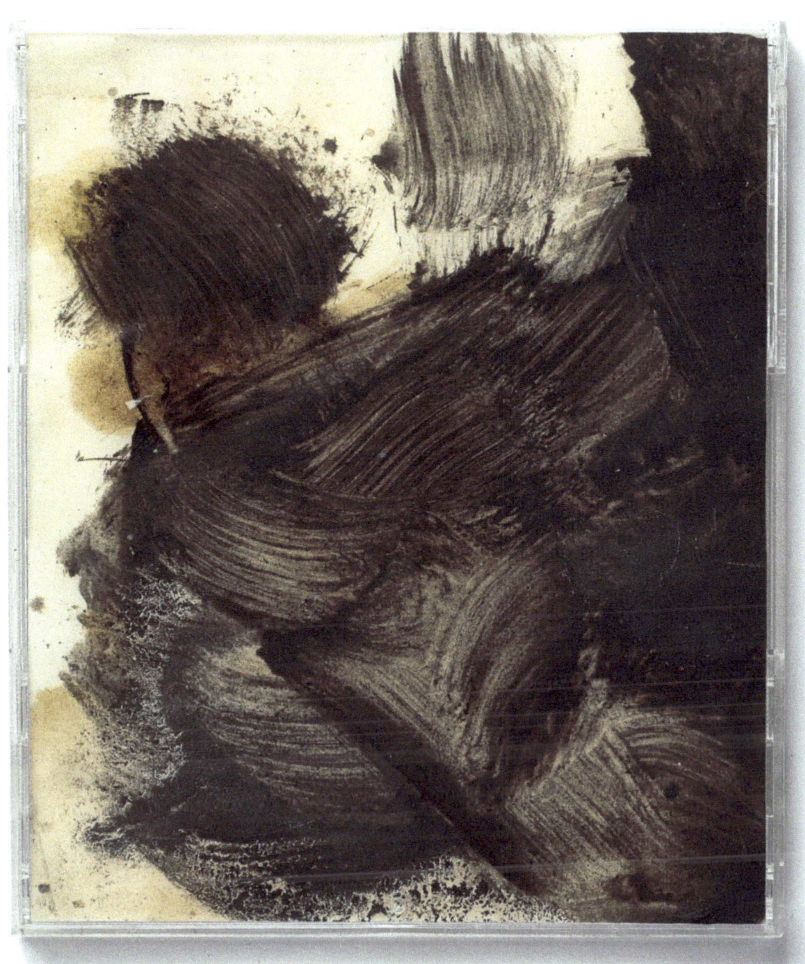

NOTES

1 S. Kierkegaard. *Sickness Unto Death,* trans. H.V. Hong and E.H. Hong (1983), adapted from pp. 35-42.

2 Samuel Beckett, *Texts for Nothing,* trans. Beckett (1974), p. 16.

3 M. Merleau-Ponty, *Signs,* trans. adapted from *R. C. McCleary* (1964), p. 117.

4 "*A rose is a rose is a rose is a rose*" from G. Stein, *Autobiography of Alice B. Toklas* (1990), p. 137.

5 Mallarmé, *Selected Poetry & Prose,* trans. M.A.C. (1982) p. 77. *cf,* Mallarmé, *Oeuvres* (1945), p. 647. "The [book] is an infinite sphere whose center is everywhere and whose circumference is nowhere." from the *Liber XXIV Philosophorum,* author anonymous.

6 Samuel Beckett, *Texts for Nothing,* trans. Beckett (1974), p. 16.

7 P. Neruda, *Twenty Love Poems and a Song of Despair,* trans. W. S. Merwin (1969), p. 89.

8 L. Wittgestein. *Tractatus Logico-Philosophicus. Routledge,* trans. D. F. Pears and B. F. McGuinness (1974), p. 89.

ACKNOWLEDGEMENTS

I am indebted to my loved ones who nourish my presence of mind; to Jonathan Bennett Bonilla for adding a further layer of meaning through his writing; to Jon Wrigley for patiently documenting each piece, and finally to Yanyun Chen and Jeremy Fernando of Delere Press for their warm affection.

VINCE BRIFFA

My deepest love and gratitude to my partner, M.A.W., who occupied the dark night *What Matter Who's Speaking* was written within.

This book could not have been written were it not for my unavowable community: *my first reader*, Kevin McIlvoy, for inhabiting the work and helping me to unwork it further; *my poet-stars,* Gabrielle Calvocoressi, Mary Leader, James Longenbach, Martha Rhodes, and Ellen Bryant Voigt; *my master-thinkers*, Giorgio Agamben, Judith Butler, Chris Fynsk, Bracha Ettinger and Siegfried Zielinski, for lending me your thinking a while; *my visual collaborator at a distance*, Vince Briffa; and finally, Yanyun Chen and Jeremy Fernando, of Delere Press, *for your fidélité.*

JONATHAN BENNETT BONILLA

VINCE BRIFFA

www.vincebriffa.com

My work centres on the co-existence of dualities. It treads blurred borders and investigates uncertain divides between opposing poles. It synthesises extremities, and acts as a seam that binds together disparate realities.

Uncertain of its own actuality, it questions its own being.

I am not a painter or sculptor, I am also not a filmmaker or a writer.

I produce 'work'.

It is my vocabulary. It is the vehicle that best embodies my thoughts and connects all my creative output.

JONATHAN BENNETT BONILLA

Jonathan Bennett Bonilla (JBB) is a PhD candidate at *The European Graduate School,* and received his MFA from The Program for Writers at *Warren Wilson College*. JBB is an Assistant Professor of English at *Middlesex Community College*, and lives in the north shore region of Massachusetts.

www.ingramcontent.com/pod-product-compliance
Lightning Source LLC
LaVergne TN
LVHW070214110826
845147LV00003B/575

* 9 7 8 9 8 1 1 1 2 6 7 2 7 *